ABRAHAM NUTR
A BETTER WAY TO

7 DAY DETOX

Recipe Book

Smoothies - Soups - Salads

ROBERT G. ABRAHAM RHNC

DISCLAIMER

The 7-Day Detox is designed for generally healthy individuals. As with any nutritional program, you should consult your licensed healthcare practitioner before beginning.

Nothing in the 7-Day Detox should be misconstrued as medical treatment or advice. The participant understands that undertaking this program is their sole responsibility of themselves and not that of the provider of the recipes.

Be advised that the recipes are not intended as a prescription for any illness or disease. Not all foods are tolerated by everyone equally. If difficulties or discomfort arise due to your inability to digest, tolerate or utilize any foods suggested, discontinue use until the reason for the difficulty can be addressed - if necessary seek appropriate medical care.

Acknowledgement

I would like to express my deepest gratitude to the NutraPhoria School Of Holistic Nutrition. Without the in-depth education and support I received, this endeavor would not have been possible.

TABLE OF CONTENTS

Introduction

Hello everyone!!! I am Robert Abraham, a Registered Health and Nutrition Counselor. In this book, I will share with you my 7-Day Detox Recipes. This plan is not intended to use past 7 days at a time but you can always return to it when you feel the need to boost your energy, improve mental clarity, support digestion, and strengthen the immune system in addition to many other benefits.

"Without Proper Diet, Medicine is of No Use.
With Proper Diet, Medicine is of No Need."

-Ancient Ayurvedic Proverb

Do You Need to Detox?

- ☐ Are you constipated, congested, and feel gassy & bloated?

- ☐ Do you feel tired, and low in energy?

- ☐ Has your hair lost it's shine, and does you skin look dull?

- ☐ Have you gained unexplained weight, despite a consistent diet?

- ☐ Do you get frequent colds, yeast infections, allergy symptoms, mouth sores, or UTIs?

- ☐ Do you feel foggy, find it difficult to concentrate, and are becoming more forgetful?

- ☐ Does your body feel itchy, achy, and/or inflamed?

- ☐ Are you experiencing decreased digestion?

- ☐ Do you have increased cravings for unhealthy foods like sugar, refined carbs & fat?

- ☐ Are you experiencing unexplained anxiety and depression symptoms?

If three or more of the above apply to you, then a detox may be just what you need to reset your body, and regain a healthy balance.

7 DAY DETOX SHOPPING LIST

Dried Herbs & Spices:

Cumin
Thyme
Rosemary
Oregano
Turmeric
Dill
Black Pepper
Himalayan Sea Salt
Bragg Sprinkle Sea Salt

Fresh Herbs:

2 Bunches organic fresh cilantro
2 Bunches organic fresh parsley

Liquids:

Almond milk (unsweetened)
Tea (peppermint, chamomile, dandelion)
8 Cups vegetable stock

Fruits & Veggies:

6 Lemons
2 Limes
2 Bulbs garlic
Fresh ginger
1 Yellow onion
1 Purple onion
4 Organic apples
1 Bag or container of organic leafy greens
4 Avocados
4 Beets

Fruits & Veggies continued:

1 Pint organic blueberries
1 Bag of frozen organic raspberries
1 Orange
2 Heads broccoli
1 Butternut squash
1 Bag carrots
1 Whole cauliflower
1 Bunch of green onion
1 Leek
2 Bunches kale
2 Bunches of dandelion greens
1 Small purple cabbage
1 Yam
3 Zucchini's
7 Cucumbers
3 Bunches Celery
1 Bag of frozen pineapple

Nuts, legumes, & Seeds:

Goji berries
Cashew
nuts
Pumpkin
seeds
Chickpeas

Oils:

Extra Virgin Olive
Oil Coconut Oil

Other:

Apple cider vinegar
Fermented wheatgrass powder
Spirulina powder
Organic miso paste

7 DAY DETOX MEAL PLAN

	BREAKFAST	SNACK / TEA	LUNCH	SNACK	DINNER
DAY 1	Upon Rising: Large glass of water with juice of 1/2 lemon *Detox Smoothie 1	Steamed broccoli with lemon juice, 1 clove crushed garlic in a drizzle of olive oil 1 Cup herbal tea	* Fresh green salad with detox friendly dressing	Organic apple 12 oz glass of filtered water with 1 tbsp fermented barley or wheatgrass	*Carrot Ginger Soup 1 Cup Chamomile tea
DAY 2	Upon Rising: Large glass of water with juice of 1/2 lemon *Detox Smoothie 2	*Carrot Ginger Soup (leftover) 1 Cup herbal tea	Tomato, cucumber & avocado salad topped with juice of 1/2 lemon, 1 tbsp olive oil, & a dash of dill	1 Cup organic fresh berries 12 oz glass of filtered water with 1 tsp spirulina	*Grilled rosemary veggies topped with a handful of chopped parsley
DAY 3	Upon Rising: Large glass of water with juice of 1/2 lemon *Detox Smoothie 3	Grilled rosemary veggies topped with a handful of chopped parsley (leftover) 1 Cup herbal tea	* Fresh green salad with detox friendly dressing	Organic apple 12 oz glass of filtered water with 1 tbsp fermented barley or wheatgrass	*Roasted Yam & Kale 1 Cup Chamomile tea
DAY 4	Upon Rising: Large glass of water with juice of 1/2 lemon *Detox Smoothie 4	Steamed broccoli with lemon juice, 1 clove crushed garlic in a drizzle of olive oil 1 Cup herbal tea	Roasted Yam & Kale (leftover)	1 Cup organic fresh berries 12 oz glass of filtered water with 1 tbsp fermented barley or wheat grass	* Fresh green salad with detox-friendly dressing 1 Cup Chamomile tea
DAY 5	Upon Rising: Large glass of water with juice of 1/2 lemon *Detox Smoothie 5	Fresh sliced veggies (unlimited) of your choice with 1/2 cup hummus 1 Cup herbal tea	Tomato, cucumber, & avocado salad topped with juice of 1/2 lemon, 1 tbsp olive oil, & a dash of dill	Organic apple 12 oz glass of filtered water with 1 tsp spirulina	*Creamy Cauliflower Soup 1 Cup Chamomile tea
DAY 6	Upon Rising: Large glass of water with juice of 1/2 lemon *Detox Smoothie 6	Creamy Cauliflower Soup (leftover) 1 Cup herbal tea	* Fresh green salad with detox friendly dressing	1 Cup organic fresh berries 12 oz glass of filtered water with 1 tbsp fermented barley or wheat grass	* Hearty Veggie Detox Soup 1 Cup Chamomile tea
DAY 7	Upon Rising: Large glass of water with juice of 1/2 lemon *Detox Smoothie 7	*Guacamole with unlimited veggies 1 Cup herbal tea	Veggie soup (leftover)	Organic apple 12 oz glass of filtered water with 1 tsp spirulina	*Power smoothie 1 Cup Chamomile tea

Health *Benefits* of
Lemon Water

Lemons contain unique flavonoid compounds that have antioxidant and anti-cancer properties

- Balances PH
- Reduces Inflammation
- Decreases Wrinkles
- Fights Throat Infections
- Purifies Blood
- Flushes Toxins
- Neutralizes Free Radicals
- Boosts Immune System
- Anticarcinogenic
- Anti-aging
- Digestive Aid
- Liver Cleanser

TIP: Squeeze 1/2 a lemon in a large glass of water & drink immediately upon rising 20 mins before other food or drink

Ingredients:

1/2 Inch knob fresh peeled ginger

1 Handful parsley

1 Apple (cored)

1/2 Cucumber

2 Cups fresh leafy greens

Juice of 1/2 lemon

2 Tbsp pumpkin seeds

1 Dash turmeric

3/4 Cup water

Place everything in blender & blend well. Add more (or less) water if needed to desired consistency.

Serves 1

OPTIONAL:
Feel free to add in your favorite plant-based protein powder to your smoothies if you want to feel full longer, and have a bit more energy for the day.

Detox Smoothie Day 1

✓ Lemons are a powerful detoxifying agent, extremely alkaline, are high in vitamin C, and provide traces of calcium, potassium, and magnesium. They support liver function, purify the blood, destroy free radicals & flush out toxins.

✓ Cucumbers are full of B vitamins, silica, and electrolytes that help build clearer, brighter skin. The vitamin C, caffeic acid, and electrolytes in cucumbers makes them great at fighting puffiness and bloating in the body.

✓ Parsley detoxifies, aids digestion, removes toxins from the body, acts as a diuretic by flushing out the kidneys, and purifies the blood. It contains vitamin A, C, and E, folate, iron, and anti-oxidants.

✓ Ginger aids in digestion, eases nausea, helps maintain proper blood circulation, improves nutrient absorption, is anti-inflammatory, strengthens immune system, and fights common respiratory problems.

Ingredients:

3/4 Cup almond milk

3/4 Cup frozen pineapple 1 Beet

2 Stalks celery

1/2 Cucumber

1 Carrot

2 Cups leafy greens

2 Tbsp pumpkin seeds

Place everything in a blender & blend well. Add water if needed to desired consistency.

Serves 1

OPTIONAL:
Feel free to add in your favorite plant-based protein powder to your smoothies if you want to feel full longer, and have a bit more energy for the day.

Detox Smoothie Day 2

✓ Beets are a powerful liver cleanser. Betanin and vulgaxanthin are two compounds in beets shown to provide antioxidant, anti-inflammatory, and detoxification support. They clean the toxins that have been removed from the liver, allowing them to be flushed out of the system instead of being reabsorbed by the body.

✓ During a detox, coconut oil can help combat candida, fungal infections, and viruses while supporting digestion.

✓ Pineapple contains bromelain, a powerful digestive enzyme that aids in digestion, and has anti-inflammatory, anti-clotting, and natural detox properties. It also contains potassium to balance electrolytes; vitamin c & manganese, which both protect cells from free radicals.

Ingredients:

1 Apple
1/2 Cup almond milk
3/4 Cup frozen pineapple
1/2 Cucumber
2 Cups leafy greens
1/2 Cup cilantro
Juice of 1/2 lemon
2 Tbsp pumpkin seeds

Place everything in blender & blend well. Add water if needed to desired consistency.

Serves 1

OPTIONAL:
Feel free to add in your favorite plant-based protein powder to your smoothies if you want to feel full longer, and have a bit more energy for the day.

Detox Smoothie Day 3

✓ Apples contain pectin, which is a soluble fiber that helps to remove food, toxins & waste from your body.

✓ Cinnamon is full of iron, calcium, and manganese, which are fantastic at helping your body process fats and keeping blood sugar in check.

✓ Pumpkin seeds are high in b-vitamins, tryptophan (which converts into mood-boosting serotonin), and zinc,
which promotes a healthy metabolism & helps fight free radicals. Zinc deficiencies can lead to fatigue and contribute to neuropsychiatric disorders such as ADHD, & depression.

Ingredients:

1 Cup dandelion greens

1 Cup kale

2 Stalks celery

1/2 Inch knob of peeled fresh ginger 1/2 Avocado

3/4 Cup water

Place everything in blender & blend well. Add more water (or less) as needed to desired consistency.

Serves 1

OPTIONAL:
Feel free to add in your favorite plant-based protein powder to your smoothies if you want to feel full longer, and have a bit more energy for the day.

Detox Smoothie Day 4

✓ Celery helps to lower high blood pressure & reduce bloating. It contains compounds that reduce inflammation & stress. Celery is also a powerful detoxifier & colon cleanser.

✓ Avocados provide healthy fats to keep you sustained longer, and a decent amount of fiber, which is excellent for keeping your digestion flowing & cleansing the colon.

✓ Dandelion greens have compounds that promote good liver and kidney function and help these organs to flush toxins from the body. It also acts like a diuretic while having a slight laxative effect, helping to cleanse the body.

Ingredients:

3/4 Cup almond milk

3/4 Cup blueberries

1/4 Cup goji berries

2 Cups leafy greens

1/2 Cup frozen pineapple

1 Tbsp coconut oil

1/2 Inch knob fresh peeled ginger Dash turmeric

Dash cinnamon

Place everything in blender & blend well. Add water as needed to desired consistency.

Serves 1

OPTIONAL:
Feel free to add in your favorite plant-based protein powder to your smoothies if you want to feel full longer, and have a bit more energy for the day.

Detox Smoothie Day 5

✓ Blueberries contain compounds that help lessen the tissue-damaging effects of chronic inflammation. They have antiviral properties & are loaded with super-detoxifying phytonutrients while also acting as antibiotics by blocking bacteria in the urinary tract, helping to prevent infections.

✓ Turmeric helps boost the liver's ability to detoxify. It also helps with inflammatory bowel disease and has antioxidant & cancer-fighting properties and there is promising research indicating possible protection against neurodegenerative diseases such as Alzheimer's.

Ingredients:

3/4 Cup water
Juice of 1 lime
1 Cup leafy greens
1 Cup dandelion greens
3/4 Cup of frozen pineapple
1/2 Cucumber
1/2 Avocado
1/4 Cup of cilantro
1/2 Inch knob fresh peeled ginger
Dash Cinnamon

Place everything in a blender &
blend well. Add more (or less)
water as needed to desired
consistency.

Serves 1

OPTIONAL:
Feel free to add in your favorite plant-based
protein powder to your smoothies if you want
to feel full longer, and have a bit more energy
for the day.

Detox Smoothie Day 6

✓ Cilantro helps detoxify heavy metals from the body by binding to toxins and loosening them from the tissue. It also contains two specific compounds which possess anti-arthritic and anti-rheumatic properties helping those with chronic inflammatory conditions.

✓ Limes can be a great flavor substitute for lemons giving your smoothie a fresh tangy taste. Like lemons, limes offer alkalizing, detoxifying benefits in the body, in addition to having a similar nutritional profile aside from being slightly lower in vitamin C.

Ingredients:

1/4 Cup goji berries

1/2 Cup frozen raspberries

1/2 Inch knob fresh peeled ginger 1 Handful parsley

1 Apple (cored)

1/2 Cucumber

1 Tbsp coconut oil

2 Cups fresh leafy greens

Juice of 1/2 lemon

1 Dash turmeric

3/4 Cup water

Place everything in blender & blend well. Add more (or less) water if needed to desired consistency.

Serves 1

OPTIONAL:
Feel free to add in your favorite plant-based protein powder to your smoothies if you want to feel full longer, and have a bit more energy for the day.

Detox Smoothie Day 7

✓ Goji berries have been used in traditional Chinese medicine for thousands of years - they are rich in antioxidants and help to repair cellular damage.

✓ The healthy fats added to smoothies such as coconut oil and pumpkin seeds help the body absorb fat-soluble vitamins such as vitamins A, E, D, and K. Other healthy fats perfect for smoothies are hemp seeds, chia seeds, & flax seeds.

Keep up with a smoothie a day after your detox ends & get creative! It is a fantastic way to get a high amount of health-boosting vitamins and minerals.

Lunch & Dinner Recipes

Any of these meals can be eaten at lunch or dinner so they have been placed in the same category

9

Ingredients:

2 ½ Cups sliced red pepper

2 ½ Cups sliced green pepper

1 Cup sliced yellow zucchini

1 Cup sliced mushrooms

1 Cups sliced green zucchini

1 Sliced onion

1 Tbsp chopped fresh rosemary

2 Tsp fresh dill

2 Tbsp chopped parsley

1 Tbsp crushed garlic

Dash of sea salt & black pepper

2 Tbsp Olive Oil

QUICK TIP:

Don't overcook. Maintain nutrients in the veggies by only lightly grilling - slightly tender but still slightly crisp

Grilled Rosemary Veggies

Mix together all ingredients and refrigerate for an hour or two. Place veggies on a grill pan over medium-high heat & cook for roughly 7 minutes until veggies are slightly tender but still crisp.

Ingredients:

2 Handfuls of leafy greens

Cucumber slices

Grated zucchini

1/2 Cup grated beet

Celery slices

Red onion slices

1/4 Cup grated carrot

Optional - fresh blueberries & chickpeas

DETOX FRIENDLY DRESSING

1/4 Cup olive oil

1/4 Cup apple cider vinegar

1 Tbsp fresh crushed garlic

1 Tsp turmeric

1 Tsp oregano

1 Tsp. thyme

1 Tbsp chopped yellow onion

1/4 Tsp sea salt

Process in food processor or blender until smooth.

Leafy Green Salad

Start with a large bed of leafy greens and add sliced cucumbers, grated zucchini, chopped green onion, 1/2 cup grated beet, celery slices, red onion slices, and 1/4 cup of grated carrots. Top with fresh blueberries & the detox-friendly dressing. The salad is 1 serving.

Store dressing 3-4 days in fridge. ** Dressing makes 4 Servings.

Ingredients:

2 Large Yams

4 Cups Baby Kale

Bragg Sprinkle

1 Tsp Olive Oil

Dressing: (make & let sit while yams are roasting)
1 Garlic Clove
1 Tsp Apple Cider Vinegar
1 Tsp Olive Oil
Dash of ground sea salt
Dash of ground pepper
1/4 tsp Dried Thyme

Serves 2

Roasted Yam & Baby Kale

Scrub yams until clean, and cut into 1/2-1 inch squares. Toss in olive oil and lay flat on a baking pan lined with parchment paper. Roast yams at 375 for 20-35 minutes. Keep an eye on them, they burn easily!

While yams are roasting, put all ingredients for the dressing in a blender or grinder & blend until smooth. Set aside. When yams are cooked, pull them out and top them with baby kale. Put the pan back in the oven & roast the yams and kale for additional 3 minutes.

Place yams & kale in a large bowl, mix in the dressing, and serve.

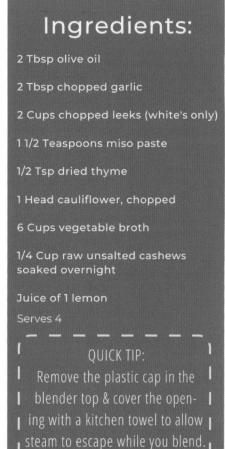

Ingredients:

2 Tbsp olive oil

2 Tbsp chopped garlic

2 Cups chopped leeks (white's only)

1 1/2 Teaspoons miso paste

1/2 Tsp dried thyme

1 Head cauliflower, chopped

6 Cups vegetable broth

1/4 Cup raw unsalted cashews soaked overnight

Juice of 1 lemon

Serves 4

QUICK TIP:
Remove the plastic cap in the blender top & cover the opening with a kitchen towel to allow steam to escape while you blend.

Creamy Cauliflower Soup

In a large saucepan, heat the oil over medium heat and saute the garlic & leeks for about 3 minutes until soft. Add cauliflower and saute for another 2 minutes. Add the vegetable broth, miso paste, thyme & lemon, and increase the heat to high, bringing it to a boil. Quickly reduce heat to medium & simmer for about 20-30 minutes, until cauliflower is tender.

Remove from heat and allow the soup to cool slightly then stir in cashews. Pour the soup into a blender in batches & puree on high for 1 - 2 minutes until smooth and creamy.

Ingredients:

1 tablespoon coconut oil

1 medium onion, chopped

4 tablespoons finely grated fresh ginger root

3 cups carrots, chopped

3 cloves garlic, crushed

1/2 medium butternut squash

8 cups chicken or vegetable stock

3 large strips of zest from an organic orange

Salt to taste

Dash of nutmeg

Chopped fresh parsley or cilantro for garnish

Serves 4

Carrot Ginger Soup

Heat the oven to 350 degrees F (175 degrees C). Scoop seeds out of the butternut squash half and place cut side down onto a greased baking sheet. Bake for 30-40 minutes, or until softened. Allow to cool, then scoop the squash flesh out of the skin using a large spoon and set aside. Discard skin. Heat coconut oil in a large pot, add the onion, 1/2 the garlic, and 1/2 the ginger, and sauté, stirring, just until the onion is translucent. Add the carrots, stock & zest. Bring to a boil, cover, reduce heat and boil gently until the vegetables are tender about 20-30 minutes. Remove the zest and discard. Add the remaining raw garlic & ginger, the nutmeg, and optional sherry. Purée the soup in batches in a blender or food processor.

Ingredients:

1 Tbsp olive oil

1 Medium yellow onion, diced

1 Leek chopped (white part)

2 Large carrots, peeled and chopped

2 Celery stalks, chopped

2 Zucchini (diced)

4 Garlic cloves, minced

1/2 Purple cabbage (chopped)

1/2 Cauliflower (chopped)

4 Cups vegetable stock

1 1/2 Tsp dried oregano

1 Tsp dried basil

1/2 Tsp dried thyme

1 Tsp sea salt

1/2 Tsp black pepper

1 Tsp Bragg Sprinkle

4 Cups of kale, stemmed and chopped

1/2 Cup fresh parsley, chopped

Serves 4

Hearty Veggie Detox Soup

Heat up a large pot over med-high heat and add olive oil. Add onion, carrots, and celery and cook for 3-5 minutes or until onions are translucent. Add in garlic & cook for 1 more minute. Poor in the vegetable stock and spices stirring well. Add chopped cabbage, cauliflower, & zucchini. Bring to a boil and then let simmer, uncovered over med-low heat for 25 minutes. Add in kale & parsley and cook for 5 more minutes until wilted.

Ingredients:

2 Avocados

3 Garlic cloves

1/4 cup cilantro

Juice of 1 lime

Dash of pepper

Dash of Himalayan sea salt

Serves 2

QUICK FACT:
Store bought guacamole often contains chemicals, coloring, inflammation causing oil, modified starches, and gums.

Guac-O-Licious!

Put everything in a food processor, or use a blending wand and process until smooth - or whatever texture you prefer.

Ingredients:

1 – 19oz or 540ml can of chickpeas

1 – 2 Cloves of garlic

1/4 Cup water

2 Tbsp apple cider vinegar

2 TBSP extra virgin olive oil

Dash sea salt

Serves 2

QUICK FACT:
Chickpeas help balance blood sugar, lower cholesterol, and blood pressure & help reduce inflammation, & cancer risk

Best Ever Hummus

Add all ingredients into a food processor and process until very smooth, scraping down a few times. The longer you process the dip....the more smooth and creamy it gets.

Store in refrigerator for up to 1 week.

My 7 Day Detox Journey

_____

_____

_____

_____

_____

_____

_____

_____

_____

_____

_____

_____

_____

_____

_____

_____

_____

_____

_____

_____

_____

_____

_____

_____

_____

_____

_____

_____

_____

_____

_____

_____

_____

_____

_____

_____

_____

_____

_____

_____

_____

_____

_____

_____

_____

My 7 Day Detox Journey

My 7 Day Detox Journey

_____

_____

_____

_____

_____

_____

_____

_____

_____

_____

_____

_____

_____

_____

_____

_____

_____

_____

_____

_____

_____

_____

_____

My 7 Day Detox Journey

_____
_____
_____
_____
_____
_____
_____
_____
_____
_____
_____
_____
_____
_____
_____
_____
_____
_____
_____
_____
_____
_____
_____
_____
_____
_____
_____

My 7 Day Detox Journey

_____
_____
_____
_____
_____
_____
_____
_____
_____
_____
_____
_____
_____
_____
_____
_____
_____
_____
_____
_____
_____
_____
_____